SCALEX

Jon Mountfort

SHIRE PUBLICATIONS

Published in Great Britain in 2012 by Shire Publications
Ltd, Midland House, West Way, Botley, Oxford OX2 0PH,
United Kingdom.
44-02 23rd Street, Suite 219, Long Island City, NY 11101,
USA.

E-mail: shire@shirebooks.co.uk • www.shirebooks.co.uk

A CIP catalogue record for this book is available from the
British Library.

Shire Library no. 572   •   ISBN-13: 978 0 74780 747 6

Jon Mountfort has asserted his right under the Copyright,
Designs and Patents Act, 1988, to be identified as the
author of this book.

Designed by Ken Vail Graphic Design, Cambridge, UK
and typeset in Perpetua and Gill Sans.
Printed in China through Worldprint Ltd.

12 13 14 15 16   12 11 10 9 8 7 6 5 4 3

COVER IMAGE
Three decades of Scalextric Formula 1 cars – Phil Hill
with the 1,500 cc V6 shark-nose Ferrari of the early 1960s,
Jackie Stewart's 3-litre V8 Tyrrell Cosworth from the
1970s, and Nigel Mansell in his turbocharged 1,500 cc
Canon Williams Honda from 1988.

TITLE PAGE IMAGE
The front page of the very first Scalextric catalogue, dated
January 1960, shows the new plastic cars. Before Tri-ang
took over they were made of tinplate.

CONTENTS PAGE IMAGE
The rear-engined Lotus chases the shark-nose Ferrari
through the Goodwood chicane. These were the cars
included with the GP33 set of 1963.

ACKNOWLEDGEMENTS
Many thanks to Steve Langford who runs the
Huntingdonshire Slot Car Club for his great support and
for lending cars and buildings, and to Andrew Fory also for
lending cars.

Photographs by Andy Jackson of A J Images and the author.

Thank you to Hornby Hobbies Ltd for kind permission to
use scans from catalogues and box artwork.

Shire Publications is supporting the Woodland Trust, the UK's leading woodland conservation charity, by funding the dedication of trees.

CONTENTS

THE EARLY YEARS

JUST LIKE THE REAL THING

THE DATE is 4 August 1957. The place is the Nürburgring, Germany's most famous motor racing circuit. In pole-position on the grid is Juan Manuel Fangio, already four times World Champion, in his Maserati. Next to him are two English drivers, Mike Hawthorn and Peter Collins in their Ferraris. The chequered flag falls, and Fangio hurtles off for what will be his last ever Formula 1 victory and a fifth world title, the Ferraris roaring after him like greyhounds after the hare.

The date is 25 December 1957. One lucky boy unwraps the paper from a large heavy box-shaped present and sees the magic word 'Scalextric' printed in large letters on the front. 'Oh wow! You got me that new toy I've heard about.' Feverishly he rips off the remaining wrapping-paper and removes the lid, probably tearing one of its corners in the rush to get at the contents. Pulling off the yellow card cover which holds in all the bits, he grabs one of the cars, a shiny scarlet Maserati. It is made of tinplate, held together with tabs and slots, just as were 50 per cent of all toys manufactured at that time. He fondles its rubber driver, featureless and without legs, then spins the rear wheels as if expecting to hear the engine burst into life. Then he takes out the Ferrari and does the same with that. He has no interest in the little booklet included with the set which comes with the tantalising title '5 minutes to go…' 'Dad!' he shrieks, 'Can you help me build it?!' 'Just give me 5 minutes son,' comes his father's reply. *Oh well*, thinks the lad, *I'll have a go at building it myself*. Ignoring the instructions, he takes the track from the box and starts putting it together on the pine-needle coated carpet… 'Did you remember to get batteries Dad?…' The Scalextric story has begun…

WHAT'S IN A NAME?

Scay-lectric is what most people call it – although some try to accommodate the 'x' that they know is present in the name by calling it *Scay-lec-trix*. 'Scalex' was a range of tinplate toys made by a company called Minimodels in Havant, Hampshire. Their creator, Bertram Francis, known as Fred, a toolmaker

Opposite:
The very first
plastic car, the
British Vanwall.
Notice the rubber
track that just
pushed together.

The first Scalextric instruction booklet was called '5 minutes to go...' and had a great picture of Fangio's Maserati on the front.

SCALEXTRIC MOTOR RACING **MANUAL**

5 minutes to go...

turned model engineer, formed Minimodels Ltd in 1947 so that he could sell his own accurate tinplate models of racing cars and sports cars such as the Jaguar XK120. Power for these models was the 'pull-back' clockwork motor. Each vehicle had a fifth wheel, which was wound up by being pulled back along the floor, powering the car forwards when it was released. When Fred Francis had his brainwave to electrify Scalex models, presumably during 1955 or '56, he retained this fifth wheel, electrically insulated it down the middle so that it could pick up positive electric current from one side and negative electric current from the other, then made it tapered and thin enough at the circumference to run in a metal slot mounted in a rubber track. When these cars were fitted with an electric motor driving the back wheels, the fifth wheel, known as a 'gimbal', both collected current from the track and steered it along the slot, the front wheels of the car merely being decoration and not contributing functionally in any way. Since the forebears of the new cars were called Scalex, and these had an electric motor, he called them 'Scalextric'.

The fifth wheel or 'gimbal', insulated between the two halves, provided both current collection and steering. The fluff around the spindle was a common affliction for all Scalextric cars.

THE FIRST SETS

Unsurprisingly, the first sets were called Set 1, Set 2 and Set 3. The first car was the Maserati 250F, which Fangio drove to victory at the Nürburgring: having been 40 seconds behind Hawthorn and Collins with ten laps to go, he proceeded to break the lap record on every subsequent lap, overtaking the two Ferraris just before the chequered flag. Set 1 contained two of these Maseratis and an oval of the extremely smelly rubber track that was used for the first six years of Scalextric's existence until replaced by the now-familiar plastic variety.

At some point during the first year, a Ferrari 4.5L became available, which would have been approximately modelled on a Tipo 801 as driven by Hawthorn and Collins, although not necessarily in the correct scarlet colour! (In fact there are only green and blue tinplate Ferraris – the author has never seen a red one other than the earlier Scalex version with the clockwork motor.) The sets were soon sold with one of each type of car.

Set 1 with its two Maseratis, cardboard battery box (top right), controller (top left) and instruction booklet. The oil bottle is next to the controller and the skid oil is next to the battery box.

The first two tinplate cars with their hand-less rubber drivers, the Ferrari in the foreground, the Maserati behind.

The shared controller – just an on/off button for each track.

For the first three years of its existence, Scalextric was available as just these sets, plus one extra car, the tinplate Austin-Healey. This was made in very small quantities, not included in any of the sets, and is now extremely rare. The main difference between the three sets was the track configuration: Set 1 had an oval track; Set 2 had a figure-of-eight with crossroads; and Set 3 had a figure-of-eight track with flyover bridge. No transformer was supplied with the sets (this didn't occur until the 1970s), but a cardboard battery holder was included. This was printed on the outside to look like a building, and power was supplied by three 4.5-volt zinc/carbon batteries. The controller (for there was only one, shared by both participants) was a tinplate box with two on/off switches, one for each track. Unbelievably, the only available control was all or nothing – full blast or stop!

If you can imagine the shiny rubber back wheels of the cars struggling for grip on the shiny black rubber of the track, you have some idea of how difficult these things were to control. But, incredibly, the Scalextric designers obviously didn't think the setup taxing enough for the skills of their drivers because they provided each set with a bottle of 'Pure Silicone skid patch fluid' to make the track just that extra bit slippery!

All sets at this time, and for quite a few years to come, were supplied with a little bottle of Shell oil with which to lubricate the axles and motor bearings. The instructions urged the amateur mechanic in the pits to apply this very sparingly, and not too often.

THE PLASTIC REVOLUTION

As often happens with ground-breaking innovations, supplying unexpected demand can be extremely difficult and Minimodels quickly ran into trouble, being taken over in 1958 by Lines Bros Ltd who traded under the familiar name of 'Tri-ang'. The heavy tinplate cars with their hard rear wheels and gimbal steering never had much grip and weren't very good at cornering, rolling out of their slot with the greatest of ease when even a minor track undulation was encountered. Lines Bros were experts in the new field of plastic toys and embarked on a complete re-design of the cars, making them much lighter and using a plastic pin to guide them in the slot. The first plastic cars were Stirling Moss's F1 Vanwall and two sports cars: the Aston Martin and the Lister Jaguar (pictured on page 17), all of which became available in 1960. The other huge improvement was the variable speed controller (a thumb-

If you required an extra level of difficulty, you just followed the instructions on the skid patch fluid.

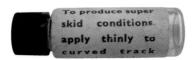

To produce super skid conditions. apply thinly to curved track

operated plunger varied the current supplied to the track), with one controller per person.

The first plastic cars are referred to as the 'big head' versions, and if you look at the illustration of the two Vanwalls (page 4) you can see why. In later versions the drivers had smaller heads with more detailing on the upper body. Tri-ang also used a different motor from the old tinplate models, the famous 'RX motor', which was the same one they used in their model railway locomotives.

The very first Scalextric catalogue, dated January 1960, was a single folded sheet of paper, giving four pages. The first page (see page 1) proudly showed off the new cars and hand controller. The second page had a whole range of buildings which you could buy to enhance your circuit, one of which, the control tower, was even available with a battery operated public address unit.

You can get some idea of the rapid progress of the toy under its new owners from the fact that Catalogue 2, produced just one year later in 1961, had twenty-four pages and boasted of four Grand Prix cars and four sports cars, one of which (the Lister Jaguar) was to be available with working front and rear lights!

New for 1961 was the 'Goodwood Chicane' (shown in several illustrations later in the book), a cunningly designed hazard which all but the expert driver had to negotiate at a snail's pace. The secret was to smack the back end of the car against the rubber Goodwood wall with just sufficient force to straighten its progress, then hope you wouldn't spin off at the next kink from which there was nothing to protect you. The two green rubber bushes serenely surveyed this scene of carnage, one of them occasionally being blasted across the room by an errant driver and his chariot.

In 1963 the heavy smelly rubber track was replaced with the lighter plastic type, called 'Plexytrack', which remained unchanged for the next forty years. This had the added advantage that each piece was locked in place with its neighbour using round lugs. The old rubber track had to be pushed together, then secured using fiddly metal 'track clips'.

TRACK AND POWER HOOK-UP

One of the many big attractions of your SCALEXTRIC Set is the "Plexytrack" —pliable, flexible and virtually indestructible

Plexytrack from 1961's Catalogue 2, demonstrating how the metal track clips should be used to keep it all together. Note how the power connections had to be inserted between the two adjoining track sections.

THE 1960s:
THE GOLDEN AGE

THE FIRST TWO CATALOGUES covered the years 1960 and 1961 and the popularity of the toy took off, so much so that Catalogue 3 used the slogan 'The Hobby That Is Fast Becoming An International Sport'. Whether this was true, or whether it was merely an encouragement for it to happen on the part of the marketing department at Tri-ang, we can't be sure. But the catalogue certainly showed a range of new and innovative products bursting forth onto every lad's wish-list.

1962

The first of these was the vintage set V3 with a couple of glorious Bentleys lumbering round the track. Interestingly, the catalogue illustration shows two green Bentleys, but the sets were actually supplied with one green and one black to make it easier to spot which was which.

Such was the detailing on these cars, and their fragility, that the instructions offered the wise advice that the mudguards were detachable and should be removed before allowing them onto the racetrack. How many little boys would have read *that* before launching them into the fray?

Also new for 1962 was motorcycle racing or, to be more accurate, sidecar racing. These were almost impossible to control. The distance from the guide pin to the rear wheels was tiny which, when added to the fact that the tyres were barely a millimetre wide, meant that even the slightest exuberance on the throttle sent them spinning round like tops. This set included the first version of the humpback bridge, complete with its rubber bridge sides, nicely hand painted with shrubs and flowers. These wonderful machines had a special design of motor all of their own that was belt driven to the back wheels using a rubber O-ring. The first 'Typhoons', as they were called, had no front wheel, just a plastic 'skid', but later ones were fitted with revolving front wheels.

The third innovation for 1962 was lighting: not only cars with lights but also trackside lights to illuminate the pits and buildings. Imagine the excitement of closing the curtains, flicking off the light-switches,

Opposite:
This beautiful illustration from Catalogue 3 shows what could be achieved by those with huge patience and deep pockets.

11

V3 set shown with two green Bentleys in the catalogue from 1962 – in the set itself one was black. The track at this time was still rubber.

The 'Bentley Boys'. Accessories at this time were made of rubber: bushes, a flexible hedge, and a 'Track Safety Barrier' – a square of moulded hay-bales ideal for standing someone on.

The motorcycle combinations, called Typhoons, hurtle across the bridge. Note the rubber track with its push-together connectors.

then watching the little blobs of headlights zooming around as if detached from their vehicles.

1963

A new range of cars and sets called 'Formula Juniors' was produced in 1963. Scalextric sets were quite expensive for the average parent, so Tri-ang came up with the idea of making a budget range that would allow the more impecunious to get a starter set for around two thirds of the cost. The sets still needed track and hand controllers, so the only thing they could save money on was the cars – and Formula Junior cars were indeed very cheap and nasty compared with the 'proper' ones.

Middle:
The Cooper and Lotus Formula Juniors. The building is the 'Racing Pit' complete with tools, refuelling rig and spare tyres, surrounded by a gathering of Scalextric figures.

Bottom left:
The cars available in 1963 along with their prices in pounds, shillings and pence.

Bottom right:
Graham Hill with his Scalextric set – one hopes that he was driving the Lotus, as he did in real life, and not the shark-nose Ferrari. This photograph was a publicity shot for the film *The Fast Lady*.

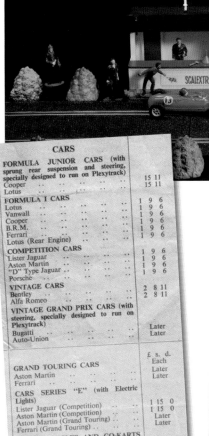

CARS			
FORMULA JUNIOR CARS (with sprung rear suspension and steering, specially designed to run on Plexytrack)			
Cooper		15	11
Lotus		15	11
FORMULA 1 CARS			
Lotus	1	9	6
Vanwall	1	9	6
Cooper	1	9	6
B.R.M.	1	9	6
Ferrari	1	9	6
Lotus (Rear Engine)			
COMPETITION CARS			
Lister Jaguar	1	9	6
Aston Martin	1	9	6
"D" Type Jaguar	1	9	6
Porsche	1	9	6
VINTAGE CARS			
Bentley	2	8	11
Alfa Romeo	2	8	11
VINTAGE GRAND PRIX CARS (with steering, specially designed to run on Plexytrack)			
Bugatti			Later
Auto-Union			Later

	£ s. d. Each
GRAND TOURING CARS	
Aston Martin	Later
Ferrari	Later
CARS SERIES "E" (with Electric Lights)	
Lister Jaguar (Competition)	1 15 0
Aston Martin (Competition)	1 15 0
Aston Martin (Grand Touring)	Later
Ferrari (Grand Touring)	Later
MOTOR CYCLES AND GO-KARTS	
Typhoon	1 9 6
Hurricane	1 9 6
Go-Kart (with steering, specially designed to run on Plexytrack)	1 9 6

The Go-Karts initially had a plastic undertray beneath the motor/axle assembly as shown in the picture, but this was soon dispensed with as it kept getting caught on the track.

The box lid for the Track & Pit Lights set has one of the nicest pieces of artwork ever produced by Tri-ang.

The year 1963 also brought model Go-Karts. These used the same small motors and rear axles as the Formula Juniors, but with tiny wheels and tyres, a nicely-modelled driver and highly detailed, accurate, chrome-plated engines. Each one had two engines, probably to make them symmetrical – although in real life of course Go-Karts had only one.

Also launched in 1963 was the CM33 set, which had the Porsche Spyder and D-type Jaguar sports cars (shown on page 26) that had been available as individual cars since Catalogue 2, and the beautiful CM34 set, which not only had cars with head and tail lights (the Lister Jaguar and Aston Martin) but also four track lights included, two of which could be clipped to the side of the road, and two with rubber suckers that could be attached to any of the range of plastic model buildings available to make the layout more realistic.

The vintage set V3 was replaced by set V33 which, instead of having two Bentleys, was now supplied with the 2.3 8c Alfa Romeo of the early 1930s in blue (illustrated on page 34), in place of the black Bentley.

Also featured in the catalogue were two new pre-war cars, one of which (the Auto Union) was produced in small but reasonable numbers, the other of which was never put into mass production at all. Apparently the C/70 Bugatti was very difficult to make and although it featured in catalogues right through to number 9, it was never available off-the-shelf in shops and the few specimens surviving change hands for thousands of pounds, even when they are not in perfect condition. The Auto Union

The Sound Effects Record was called 'roar!' and offered a Long Race or a Short Race on side one for Grand Prix cars, and likewise on side two for TT motorcycles.

had the interesting colour scheme of yellow body and green wheels (the real-life car was silver).

To wrap up the innovations from 1963, there was the 'Fuel Load Gauge', an irritating device that reduced the performance of your car at the beginning to simulate the effects of a full tank of fuel, then allowed flat-out speed just as the petrol ran out and you suddenly ground to a halt.

You could also enjoy the 'Sound Effects Record', on vinyl of course, with noises of cars and motorcycles in both long and short races. Unfortunately there weren't any crashes to be heard, so the outcome was never true to real Scalextric life. The much better 'twin auto-screams' was produced in 1965, an electronic box that generated engine sounds according to how the driver pressed the plunger on the hand controller.

The left-hand-drive Hurricanes, shown here in all the four colours in which they were produced. In the background is the TV tower – this is the earlier version with a nicely moulded set of hay-bales in the base.

15

In 1963 the Typhoon motorcycle was joined by a foreigner, the left-hand-drive Hurricane. This had a proper front wheel from the start: there are no Hurricanes with front skids.

1964

The previous year's catalogue had advertised two new cars that didn't really become available in numbers until 1964. They were supplied individually and in a set, and a true classic was born. The Set 60 with lights would have been every boy's dream – but I suspect that at £8 15s 0d (equivalent to approximately £265 at 2009 prices) not many were fortunate enough to get one. The cars were the Aston Martin DB4 (in either British Racing Green or red) and the Ferrari 250GT (in either scarlet or blue). They were held together with screws rather than the plastic catches on previous cars and seemed to be made to a higher standard, although the bumpers were prone to snapping off during high-speed impacts with the skirting board, or even just by clipping them on the white plastic track barriers. They were very heavy and so not particularly manoeuvrable, but they looked stunning.

A wonderful variant of the lighted Aston Martin DB4 was produced in 1964 – moulded in jet-black plastic, it had MARSHAL written on each door, a working light on the roof, and two white flags pushed into holes in the front and rear bumpers.

Four-lane racing also appeared in Catalogue 5. The Set 80 had four cars, four hand controllers, just about enough track to make a four-lane oval, and was even more expensive than the Set 60. The cars in the Set 80 were the poor quality formula juniors, by now re-badged as a BRM and a Porsche, so you were really better off buying decent cars and track separately.

Perhaps the highest quality cars ever produced, the Aston Martin DB4 sails above the Ferrari 250GT in their national racing colours of green and red.

The Aston Martin Marshal's car is seen helping out at the scene of a wreck against the Goodwood wall. The car in trouble is the Lister Jaguar which was the first to be fitted with working lights in 1961.

Also new this year were two sports cars, which were constructed in a completely new way – the Austin-Healey 3000 and the Mercedes 190SL. The difference was that they had no floor – the motor was snapped tightly into locating lugs in the upper body shell, as were the front and rear axles, so they were very light. They also had slick tyres for extra grip and were very nippy round the bends.

Track was now made with even larger radius corners to enable six-lane racing, while an electrically operated lap recorder counted how many circuits each car managed to make. This piece of apparatus may not have worked, or was too expensive, because it was abandoned the year after, replaced by a simple mechanical device.

1965

About the only thing that was actually different in 1965 was the launch of the model of the Mini Cooper. Of course, the full-size Mini was by this time a national icon, driven by pop stars and paupers, doctors and district nurses. One of its main features was its front-wheel drive, so the Scalextric engineers made a valiant attempt to reproduce this concept in a slot-car. The problem was interesting. The braids which pick up the electricity from the track need to be in contact with the steel conductors at all times, so they need to push down with some force, which lifts the front of the car up. But if the front

The lack of a floor made the Healey and Mercedes lighter than the DB4 and Ferrari 250, and they hugged the track better.

The front-wheel-drive Minis. Notice that the pickup braids extend quite a way in front of the car in order to prevent the front driving wheels from lifting off the track.

wheels are to be used to drive the car, these also need to be pushed down, not up, so they can gain some grip. So the two separate and vital parts of the system, both at the front of the car, required good contact with the road.

The solution was to put the braids and guide pin on the end of springy brass strips which projected about 1cm in front of the car. The owner bent the springs so that the braids made contact, and if it was just about right, the car would grip enough to be driveable. This idea was largely unsuccessful, and was abandoned two years later, when Scalextric Minis became rear-wheel-drive!

The Set 60 was demoted to Set 55 in 1965, the Aston Martin and Ferrari now being announced as 'cars without lights'. (No-one seems to have told the person designing the artwork for Catalogue 6, as Set 55 is shown with a beautifully rendered pair of cars with headlights roaring around a darkened circuit.)

The Set 55 illustration from Catalogue 6.

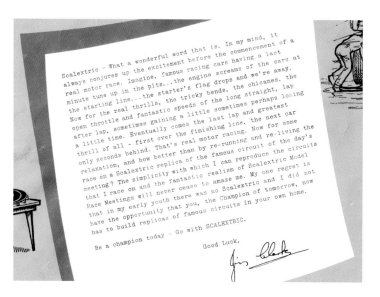

Jim Clark's introduction to the 1966 catalogue.

Scalextric - What a wonderful word that is. In my mind, it always conjures up the excitement before the commencement of a real motor race. Imagine, famous racing cars having a last minute tune up in the pits...the engine screams of the cars at the starting line...the starter's flag drops and we're away. Now for the real thrills, the tricky bends, the chicanes, the open throttle and fantastic speeds of the long straight, lap after lap, sometimes gaining a little sometimes perhaps losing a little time. Eventually comes the last lap and greatest thrill of all - first over the finishing line, the next car only seconds behind. That's real motor racing. Now for some relaxation, and how better than by re-running and re-living the race on a Scalextric replica of the famous circuit of the day's meeting? The simplicity with which I can reproduce the circuits that I race on and the fantastic realism of Scalextric Model Race Meetings will never cease to amaze me. My one regret is that in my early youth there was no Scalextric and I did not have the opportunity that you, the Champion of tomorrow, now has to build replicas of famous circuits in your own home.

Be a champion today - Go with SCALEXTRIC.

Good Luck,

Jim Clark

1966

In the world of real motor racing, 1965 was the year of Jim Clark, who won the Formula 1 World Championship, the Formula 2 World Championship, and the Indianapolis 500 in America. Scalextric already had his face on the cover of the 1965 catalogue, so it is not surprising that they utilised his fame to the full in Catalogue 7, with an introduction on the first page signed by the great driver himself. Jim Clark was much more than just an advertising gimmick: he was an ambassador for the toy, giving his time freely, and he genuinely loved Scalextric. The whole workforce was devastated when they learnt he had died in a crash at Hockenheim.

When the youngsters of 1966 flicked through the new catalogue, hearts may have skipped a beat when they realised that all their treasured cars were now obsolete. And the reason for this? 'Race-tuned'. The cars all looked the same, except for an all-important sticker applied to the side which proclaimed their new power and racing pedigree and, in all but a few cases, (the Auto Union was an exception), a black-and-white racing stripe applied to their bonnets/noses.

The famous 'Race-tuned' sticker applied to all the new cars which had the black-sided race-tuned motor and blade guide.

The differences to the mechanics of the cars were twofold. Firstly, the motors had different windings which meant that they consumed twice as much current, so much so that they had to have new Race-tuned hand controllers, as using the new cars with the old controllers first made them very hot and smelly, and then completely melted them.

The Race-tuned Cooper (red) and BRM (green) were easily distinguishable by the black and white racing stripe applied down the length of the bonnet.

Secondly, the guide pin now became the guide blade, moved to the very front of the car and pivoted so that it could follow the track. This change actually made more difference than the motors, and was an innovation which has remained unaltered into the twenty-first century.

Not content with just six-lane racing, another large radius corner became available in 1966 to enable eight-lane racing, ideal for the many slot-car racing clubs that were springing up all over the world. The shallow curves gave drivers the chance for some serious high-speed cornering without the cars falling off the track. Most people will remember the incredibly tight inside lane of the innermost right-angle corner which was always a nightmare to negotiate (as illustrated with the Ford Mirage and Ferrari P4, page 40).

1966 was the launch year of the biggest Scalextric set yet – the monstrously expensive Set 90 cost £15 8s 0d – about £450 at 2009 prices. This was a very peculiar set because it had four cars, but only two hand controllers and a two-lane track. The idea was that you either raced two

The race-tuned Auto Union does not have a stripe on its nose, but its white colour more accurately replaces the previous yellow version.

sports cars against each other (Austin-Healey 3000 in green and Mercedes 190SL in blue), or you raced the two Formula 1 cars which were also supplied in the set (Cooper in red and Lotus in green, both of which were Formula Juniors). Because of its expense at the time, this is a very rare set nowadays, but the cars are common because they were sold separately.

1968

Skipping 1967 for the moment (the star of that year is covered in the chapter on film and television), we arrive in 1968 and the launch of the ultimate handling machine: the 'Power Sledge'. The idea was that the body was superfluous to any slot-car. All you needed was the pick-up bolted onto the front of the motor, and the driving wheels attached directly to the rear. Bodies could then simply be clipped onto the rear axle bearings.

From 1966 you could buy the official Brooch (just 20mm wide and 10mm tall) to proclaim your affection for all things Scalextric.

Of course, the Power Sledge car actually went faster with the body removed, but it didn't look very pretty – a piece of steel flashing round the track in a high-speed blur, the only thing able to keep up with it being another similarly body-shorn Power Sledge. When you finally found the limit of one of these devices, it didn't simply slide off the track and bounce across the carpet – it leapt up off the banking, cart-wheeled through the air and hit the wall about 3 feet up from the ground. Due to the fact that they were so low and grey and blended in perfectly with the carpet, they gave rise to the classic Scalextric injury of the period: the painful impression of an RX motor in the sole of the shoeless foot...

Initially, only two bodies were made for the Power Sledge: the Panther and the Europa Vee. They were not based on genuine prototype racing cars,

For 1968 the four-lane Set 80 became 'Power Sledged'. Two Panthers in red and yellow head the two Europa Vees in green and white under the original rubber version of the Dunlop bridge.

21

The Monte Carlo Mini getting attention from an array of Scalextric figures – notice its roof-mounted spotlight.

but represented a sort of general, all-purpose Formula 1 car, used in a lot of the sets.

In 1968, Scalextric finally gave up on the front-wheel-drive Mini and produced a superb rear-wheel-drive version in Monte Carlo Rally livery including a spotlight on the roof.

Another big change occurred in 1968. Until that year, the variable speed hand controllers for the normal non-Race-tuned cars had all been operated using the thumb. 1968 was the year when the new design of pistol-grip finger-operated controller replaced them. The Race-tuned hand controllers had been of this design from their inception two years before, but now this style became universal.

SUPER 124

The standard scale of Scalextric cars and accessories was 1/32. The 1968 catalogue announced a new larger scale of 1/24. Of course this meant that the cars and track were a lot bigger, and hence more expensive. Not many people will have seen, let alone owned or handled, any of this luxury equipment which was really aimed at slot-car racing clubs. The track was three-lane as standard, 12 inches wide with stainless steel conductors so it could be used outdoors, and the cars were beautifully made, some even having front wheel braking systems (these were badged as ACE). Due to the high price, not many were sold. For example, the Formula 1 cars (Lotus and Ferrari) cost £4 9s 6d (equivalent to £130 in 2009). Only two other cars were made – the Alfa Romeo sports saloon and the E-type Jaguar. The cheapest set was £22 10s 0d (about £650 in 2009). By the twelfth catalogue of 1971, Super 124 was dead.

1969

The year 1968 had seen the first set which included Race-tuned cars – the Grand Prix 75 set had a Cooper and a BRM (illustrated on page 20). These old-fashioned looking cars (they were based on front-engined Formula 1 designs from the 1950s) lasted only one year: by 1969 the cars in this set were a brand new Power Sledge Lotus and Power Sledge Ferrari, both with aerofoils, a new-fangled device which had appeared on the real cars the year before. The Lotus would have been driven by one of those all-time British heroes Jim Clark or Graham Hill. As both of them had won at Indianapolis (Clark 1965, Hill 1966) the Scalextric Power Sledge Lotus was called the 'Lotus Indianapolis'.

The lovely Power Sledge Lotus and Power Sledge Ferrari flash past the TV camera on its tower. These were the first Scalextric cars produced with aerofoils.

Late in 1968 and then into 1969, a range of cars was produced in Britain that no longer used the faithful RX motor with its exposed armature, brushes and magnet. The 'can-type' motor was much shorter and, as its name suggests, enclosed in a thin steel can. The first of these cars were the Javelin and Electra (not based on real cars) followed by the Ford GT (loosely based on a GT40), a Ferrari P4, a Ford Mirage and the Lamborghini Miura. (Note that some models had been produced with can motors in Hong Kong since 1966, see chapter on overseas models.)

The can motor was much lighter than the old RX and the cars, made of just a thin sheet of plastic without a floor pan, weighed far less than previous designs. Coupled with their wide tyres, the driving experience was completely different. The acceleration was more like that of a modern slot-car, and full throttle could only be used in short bursts.

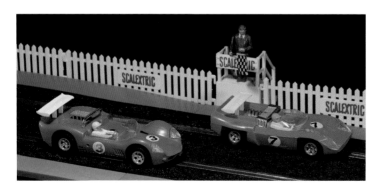

The first British-made cars to have 'can' motors, here are the Javelin and Electra in their later form with aerofoils.

23

BUILDINGS, FIGURES AND ACCESSORIES

M ANY SCALEXTRIC BUILDINGS were produced right from the very beginning in the 1950s. Probably the most common of these is the Racing Pit which was illustrated in the very first instruction manual ('5 minutes to go...') that was supplied with the tinplate sets. It was made from a cream/white plastic with brown roof and forecourt planking and a green counter-top. It was supplied with a set of flags and numbers to cut out. The Pit Accessories had to be purchased separately and consisted of a refuelling hose, a toolbox, a hammer, a vice, a fuel can, a funnel and some spare tyres. The latter were the normal treaded variety in the early years but then wide slicks were substituted, which could be made to fit on the sports cars. This made them look racier, and often necessitated cutting away the wheel arches.

The first people figures were shown in Catalogue 2 from 1961. There was a set of six Track Officials and Pit Crew, and another set of six Spectators and Press Photographers, all of which were supplied hand painted. The variation in colour schemes used on the people is wide ranging as you can see from looking at the pictures throughout this book. The following year, two more sets were added: Mechanics and Drivers; and Vendors and Spectators.

In 1966 the HP/1 Extension Pack became available. This provided a range of track, accessories and figures including a humpback bridge, a start/finish banner, the starter on his rostrum, fencing with flagpoles and a gate, six black-and-white hurdles as supplied with the later version of the Goodwood chicane, the Pit Accessories Set which included all the tools and tyres to accompany the Racing Pit building, two sheets of flags to cut out, and the two sets of figures shown on page 26.

The Starter on Rostrum was fitted with a piece of string which, when tugged, made his arm move up and down. A hole in his hand held a pin to which his flag could be attached, as can be seen in several of the pictures.

One of the nicest buildings from this early period was the Refreshment Kiosk, which had a chrome-plated tea/coffee boiler, transparent displays for all the sandwiches and cakes, and a printed backdrop showing the menu, along with shelves of drinks and other goodies.

Opposite:
The massive control centre was only ever supplied as an unmade kit of parts. The cars are the Renault RS01, the Tyrrell 008.

25

Above left: The Racing Pit and Pit Accessories Set: vice, hammer, toolbox, fuel can, funnel and spare tyres, pictured with the Porsche Spyder and D-type Jaguar sports cars.

Above: The Refreshment Kiosk with part of the roof removed so it is possible to see the detail inside. A Cooper and a Lotus from Set 80 of 1966–7.

Middle: These are the figures included in the HP/1 Extension Pack: the Track Officials and Pit Crew (left), and the Vendors and Spectators (right). In the centre is the Starter on Rostrum and Start/Finish Banner.

Left: From left: TV Camera and Crew Set (later version with plain plastic base), Entrance Building, Control Tower, Starter on Rostrum and Event Board with Hut, together with four very colourful shark-nose Ferraris.

In 1964, some buildings were produced in plastic kit form, so that children could enjoy the experience of assembling and gluing. Among these kits, the most impressive was the Control Centre, a giant edifice that was never sold in made-up form. It looked a bit like a three-tier wedding cake. It had two verandas with railings on which to stand your figures, surmounted by a clock and flagpole, and was an impressive centrepiece for any large layout.

The range of buildings and people continued more or less unchanged through until 1971 when Lines Brothers was forced into liquidation and the Scalextric brand was sold off (as described in the chapter on the 1970s). After a gap of seven years, the Grandstand and the Racing Pit (now called a Pit Stop) were reintroduced in Catalogue 19 of 1978 using the same moulds but in a super-vibrant bright orange colour. The tool kit for the pit was now supplied with the building, and so were the pit crew figures, and also the seated figures for the grandstand, but the people were no longer ready-painted.

A feature of many British racing circuits in the 1950s and '60s was the Dunlop bridge, formed in the shape and colour of a tyre, used as a pedestrian walkway to cross from the inside to the outside of the track and vice versa. The original Scalextric version of this bridge was made of rubber. It was very large and heavy and was also nicely made (see page 21). It was not until 1982 that a plastic Dunlop bridge was produced to replace the old one. It was much smaller than before – only about half the size – and moulded in bright yellow, a colour which was also used for the Pit Stop and the Grandstand from this time. However, it did have the steps and walkway included, so the figures could stand on top for a good view of the action.

Almost all the buildings and figures up to 1988 used the same designs as the old 1960s originals (an exception being the Dunlop bridge as we have seen). In 1990 and 1991 a range of new buildings was produced, the most impressive of which were the Control Tower and Crosswalk Kit, which looked like a bridge on a motorway service station, and the Start Light Post, a gantry covered in flashing red, yellow and green lights to simulate the starting system used on the real Grand Prix races.

The later version of the Scalextric Grandstand in garish orange, shown here with the Chevrolet Corvette Stingray and Ford Mustang 'Dragsters'.

FILM AND TELEVISION

IN THE EARLY YEARS, Scalextric didn't cash in on the popularity of films and television by bringing out TV- and movie-related sets. It was 1967 before the first one was released, but what a set it was! The names James Bond, Sean Connery, and the number 007 were household words by this time.

James Bond's Aston Martin was actually a DB5 in *Goldfinger*, but the faithful Scalextric DB4 was used in the set (they do look almost identical). It was moulded in white, as they couldn't manage silver in those days, and was hugely modified to provide a working ejector seat and bullet-proof shield. The activator for the ejector seat was a plastic trigger just below the door pillar. The bullet-proof shield was concealed in the boot – it popped up when another car clouted the back bumper.

The bad guys' car was a jet black Mercedes 190SL. It had a spring arrangement beneath the car at the back which, when the rear bumper was clobbered, catapulted the vehicle up in the air and flipped it over. In addition, the track was supplied with a crossover and a long curved chicane, so there was plenty of scope for the cars to come into contact.

A special 'rock' (it was actually a knobbly bit of plastic) was located so it could rotate in the centre of one of the pieces of track, and when the Aston drove past, it sometimes, depending on the glancing blow, activated the lever on the side of the car which fired the ejector seat, sending James himself up into orbit along with the car's sun roof (these are quite rare now and there are many reproduction ones about).

A friend of the author who, as a young lad, worked in a toy shop in the '60s said the sets were so fragile that, after Christmas, about half of them were returned because the cars had 'broken'.

Incredibly, it was another seventeen years before the next TV- or film-related set was released. This was 'the Amazing Spider-Man Web Racer Set' launched in Catalogue 25 of 1984.

The cars were two Triumph TR7s, one red and one yellow, suitably adorned with web designs and Spider-man motifs. The track was moulded in white. For some reason, the white track was more brittle than the normal

Opposite:
The brightly coloured TR7s of the Spider-man set stand out against the white track.

The ejector seat in operation – the sun roof having flown off first to make way for the sky-bound passenger. For some reason, James Bond himself is the one being launched into the air.

Surrounded by bad guys with guns, James Bond engages them in a shoot-out through the open sun roof of his Aston Martin.

Below:
The cars from the Knight Rider sets – a Datsun 260Z and K.I.T.T.

black (which was almost indestructible) so the lugs were prone to snapping off in the Web Racer set.

Just three years later, two fantastic Knight Rider sets were launched: one with a simple figure-of-eight track was called the 'Pursuit Mode' set; the other with a flying leap was called the 'Turbo Boost' set. The flying leap consisted of a gap where the flyover bridge would ordinarily be: you had to adjust the speed of your car precisely to clear the ravine – too slow and you dropped into the gap – too fast and you cleared the specially designed barriers which safely caught the car on landing and guided it back into its slot. One of the cars was K.I.T.T. – the futuristic computerised Pontiac Firebird TransAm from the TV series (which stood for 'Knight Industries Two Thousand'). The other car was a metallic blue Datsun 260Z, although it was labelled on the box lid as a 240Z.

The other TV related set from this 1987–8 period was M.A.S.K. – a cartoon animation produced in Japan where the forces of good (Mobile Armored Strike Command) battle the evil of VENOM (Vicious Evil Network of Mayhem). The cars were a MASK Thunderhawk and a VENOM Manta and again there were two sets, one with a flying leap and one without.

The next in this series of famous TV spin-offs was the iconic Batman. Complete with Batmobile and the Joker's Porsche Carrera, this too was available with or without the flying leap ('Batman Leap' and 'Batman Chase').

The next year, Teenage Mutant Hero Turtle sets appeared, with the individuals on their skateboards. Later TV- and film-related sets are mostly in the smaller scale 1/64 track gauge and include The Simpsons and Transformers.

Above left:
Get the speed just right and the Joker and Batmobile clear the flying leap, being guided back into their slots on landing by the chevron barriers.

Above:
Raphael shows off on his propeller-powered skateboard, skimming along the special green-coloured track which was supplied with these sets.

ÉPREUVE 4

MANCHE 3

8	ASTON MARTIN
5	VANWALL
1	COOPER
6	JAGUAR

K·L·G

OVERSEAS MODELS

R IGHT FROM the very start of their involvement in Scalextric in the early 1960s, Lines Brothers looked to sell their new toy to the large European market. In those days, before there was a free market for goods in Europe, protectionism and import duties ruled, so to get products into the countries concerned, companies either had to set up a factory on their territory, or give a licence to an existing company. Scalextric did both.

FRANCE

In 1961 they built a factory in Calais. This was a wholly owned subsidiary of the parent English company Lines Brothers, so the French boxes have 'Lines Frères S.A.' written on them. To start with, the facility on the north coast of France made the same cars that were produced approximately 100 miles due west in Havant on the south coast of England using the exact same moulds, but with the Made in England imprint blanked out. Later, the French factory made its own moulds, which were subtly different, so the parts are not interchangeable with English cars, and they also used metric threads on the screws.

After a while the Calais factory designed and built its own cars, and there was an agreement with the parent company that some of these should be made available in Britain. Catalogue 9 of 1968 featured the French-built Alpine Renault and Matra Jet sports cars shown (opposite page). They also made the trackside buildings with French wording on them.

The French versions of the English cars often had unusual colour variations – for example the French vintage Alfa Romeo was bright yellow instead of blue, while the French Bentleys had tan-coloured tonneau covers and red wheels. These strange varieties are now sought after by collectors.

When Lines Bros went into receivership in 1971, the French factory passed to Meccano France, who continued to make slot-cars with the Scalextric name under licence, although they became less and less compatible over the years and after a complete redesign in 1979 the French cars could no longer be used on standard Scalextric track. The French operation finally closed around 1981.

Opposite:
This picture shows the Matra Jet (white) and the Renault Alpine passing the French version of the Event Board and Hut.

The French
produced their
own artwork with
consummate Gallic
flair, as shown on
the box-lid of the
Alpine Renault and
Matra Jet set.

The French Bentleys
with their light
brown tonneau
covers and red
wheels. The easiest
way to spot if they
are genuine is to
check the hub-cap
of the spare wheel –
it should be a
different shape from
the ones on the
road wheels.

The English and
French Alfa Romeos
are distinctly
different!

SPAIN

In 1962 Lines Bros did a deal with the Spanish company Exin, which gave them the rights to sell Scalextric in Spain and Portugal, something which the British company could never do directly while Spain was ruled by General Franco. Under the terms of this agreement Exin were allowed to make everything except the cars in their own factory in Spain. Within a couple of years the Spanish factory was designing and manufacturing its own cars, the first of which was the tiny little Seat 600, which was released to the Spanish market in 1966. This car, re-badged as a Fiat 600, found its way into the ninth edition British catalogue of 1968, along with the lovely Mercedes 250SL sports saloon, which was also made by the Spanish firm.

When Lines Brothers sold Scalextric in 1971, the British cars went downhill rapidly, being of low quality and produced as cheaply as possible. Exin, however, did the opposite. They continued to design and make models with very fine detail and built to high quality standards – during the whole of the 1970s, there is no doubt that the best Scalextric cars in the world were being made in Spain. A good example of Spanish excellence at this time is the six-wheel Tyrrell P34, which was (and still is) an iconic Formula 1 car – nothing looked like it before or since, and it actually won one race, the Swedish Grand Prix of 1976, in the hands of Jody Scheckter. The P34 was never listed in any of the UK catalogues, but there are plenty of examples about and they are beautifully made. Exin also had a factory in Mexico so some of the Spanish cars, including the P34, were made there. Other Spanish highlights from this period are the Mustang and Corvette dragsters (illustrated on page 27), superbly decorated with striking decals, chrome everywhere and produced in just about all the colours of the rainbow.

The six-wheel Tyrrell P34 was available in many different colours (as shown here) and was manufactured in Spain or Mexico.

Exin made the unique rough terrain sets with four-wheel-drive vehicles and special hinged pickups that could follow the steep hills. This is a Puch Pinzgauer vehicle used for Africatours.

Later on, the Spanish brought out the Super Track System (STS) of four-wheel-drive off-road vehicles and sets. The motor is mounted diagonally in the base, driving both front and rear axles through skewed helical gears, a masterpiece of engineering. The pickup braids are mounted on the end of a long lever. This is hinged at the rear, allowing the vehicle to climb and descend steep hills and ravines while the braids stay in contact with the conductor rails, which remain level with the base of the track.

The Ford Mirage and Lamborghini Miura that were made in the USSR.

The Exin company continued producing Scalextric cars right through into the 1980s when the English company went through another crisis and sale, this time in a management buyout. However, even the Spanish were not immune from the financial pressure produced by the advent of electronic and video games, and the slot-car business was sold in 1993 to Tyco, and then again in 1998 to TecniToys. Now, under the SCX brand name, they are still one of the biggest producers in the slot-car market.

MANUFACTURE IN OTHER COUNTRIES
Moving away from Europe, some of the 'English' cars of the 1960s were made in Hong Kong, examples being the Triumph TR4, Sunbeam Tiger, and AC Cobra. Two, the Lamborghini Miura and Ford Mirage were even produced in Russia. They have 'Made in USSR' written on the bottom and the colour tone is much duller than the British manufactured versions of the same models.

The Australian factory that produced Scalextric under licence was called Moldex. It was noted for some of the strange colour schemes they applied to some of the cars, much to the parent company's annoyance. Their most striking feature though was the 1960s-style thumb-operated hand controllers in green and yellow, as shown in the picture (see below).

The Australian sets were made by Moldex and many had the distinctive yellow and green hand controllers shown in the top right of the picture. These cars are AC Cobras.

THE 1970s:
THE CARS GET LOWER,
THE TYRES GET FATTER

YOU STEER

THE FRONT COVER of Catalogue 11 proudly introduced a new concept for the new decade of the 1970s: 'You Steer – with power steering'. Unfortunately, this new device steered the company nowhere. The idea was that instead of merely concentrating on beating your opponent while attempting to keep your own car in its slot, you now had obstructions placed on the track, to the left and the right, which were to be avoided by turning a little steering wheel on the hand controller. There were only two positions – fully left and fully right – so the cars couldn't go straight down the middle of the track, which definitely felt odd. But the main problem was that, in order to execute one of these manoeuvres, the motor in the car had to stop, change direction, and get up to full rpm again, just to keep the car moving. By the time you had steered, the thing stuttered so badly that it had lost half its speed. Then the same procedure had to be repeated all over again to clear the next hazard. Luckily, the track supplied with the You Steer sets was identical to the normal variety, so most people just binned the cars and hazards and carried on with normal cars in the old-fashioned way.

By the thirteenth catalogue of 1972, You Steer went the same way Super 124 had done a year earlier: it was dead. Unlike Super 124, it was unlamented.

JUMP JOCKEY

You Steer was not the only innovation for 1970. A whole new concept arrived, probably with the intention of making sets more attractive for the 50 per cent of the population who had never bought Scalextric: the girls! Electric horse racing (actually called steeple-chasing in the catalogue because these things really could tackle jumps) disappeared as fast as it came: by 1971 it was no more.

THE LIQUIDATION AND SALE OF LINES BROS LTD

Did 'You Steer' and 'Jump Jockey' cost too much to develop? Their sales were certainly disappointing, but it was actually the massive investment in the

Opposite:
The Mini got a chequer-patterned roof in 1974 – and very striking it looked too. This is the later version of the Goodwood chicane with plastic green wedge and black-and-white trellis.

The You Steer gearbox unit could be purchased separately to enable the owner to convert some models of Scalextric car. Note the screw thread at the back, which moved the pickup arm to the left or right to steer the car.

Super 124 system which killed the company – by the time it was released, enthusiasm for slot-car racing clubs had collapsed and there was no market for it. In 1971 Lines Bros Ltd called in the official receiver who soon found a buyer for their Rovex Tri-ang Ltd subsidiary, which owned both Scalextric and Hornby Railways. The buyer was an English company that had previously bought the UK operation of the huge American Marx toy manufacturing company, hence its name, Dunbee-Combex-Marx Ltd. The new owners did not spend much money on development, probably wisely, so the cars of the '70s were cheaply made and not very detailed. They stopped production of

You Steer sets had special obstacles, like the one shown here in the middle of the road. The Ford Mirage and Ferrari P4 from the YS400 set are shown.

Maddest wings: the March Ford 721 (red) had a front wing which floated gracefully above the nose, completely obscuring the driver's view of the track. The Spanish-made Sigma (orange) simply had one giant wing right above his head.

all the buildings and cut the range of cars down to just eighteen models. There was now no way to create an authentic racing circuit with a TV Tower, a First Aid Hut or a Le Mans Start, but at least the core survived, along with, thankfully, the name.

STAR CARS OF THE 1970s

The best Scalextric cars at this time in terms of quality and range were undoubtedly those being made by the Spanish Exin factory, with beautiful models such as the Tyrrell P34 six-wheeler and the Mustang and Corvette Dragsters.

The early to middle 1970s saw virtually no new products released by the English factory, which was now in Margate, Kent, sharing facilities with Hornby trains, the original factory in Havant, Hampshire, having been closed during the financial crisis of 1970. The range at this time included the Javelin

The Scalextric Ford Escort rally car was badged as a Mexico and had working headlights. Here are three of them in various liveries.

The Elf Tyrrell receiving attention in the pits. This is one of the most common Scalextric cars ever made and must have been owned by tens of thousands of youngsters.

and Electra and all the other cars which had previously been You Steer, four Grand Prix cars including the JPS Lotus and Ferrari 312, a Porsche 917 and the Mercedes Wankel, plus a few others, one of which, the March Ford 721, is pictured (page 41) next to the Sigma, a car that was being produced by the Spanish factory at the same time, but was never sold in Britain.

The first really significant new car to be launched under the new ownership was the Ford Escort Mexico in 1974, the real-life version having so much success at that time in world rallying. This was accompanied the same year by a redesign of the Mini in yellow or red with a gaudy chequered roof, first in the usual Mini shape (1974), then in Clubman form (1976).

As a new crop of rising stars came to the fore in Formula 1 – for example, Emerson Fittipaldi, Niki Lauda and James Hunt – Scalextric gave us models of their cars so that we could dice with the greats on the kitchen floor, just as they were doing each week on the scorching tarmac of the world's circuits.

The Ferrari 312T and McLaren M23 Formula 1 cars with Niki Lauda and James Hunt racing neck-and-neck for the finish. After 1978 the McLaren was produced without the Marlboro logos.

Some of the most common cars that sold in large numbers at this time were the Elf Tyrrell Ford released in 1976, the Marlboro McLaren M23 released the year after, and the JPS Lotus 77 of the following year.

The first new sports/saloon cars for some years were the Datsun 260Z of 1975, shown in the photograph of the Knight Rider set (page 30), the Porsche Turbo 935 (1977), the BMW turbo 320 and Triumph TR7 (both 1978).

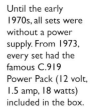

Also in 1978, the interestingly styled March six-wheeler hit the shops. This was based on an experimental Formula 1 car which never actually raced, but Scalextric liked the look of it and bought the rights to make it in model form. It was actually a great publicity success for the March company, keeping its name in the limelight for years. In 1979 Scalextric teamed it up with the JPS Lotus to be sold as a 400 Set.

Until the early 1970s, all sets were without a power supply. From 1973, every set had the famous C.919 Power Pack (12 volt, 1.5 amp, 18 watts) included in the box.

In 1978 the Triumph TR7 and a bright red BMW Turbo 320 appeared. Here they are, leaping over the scenery before crashing into each other, luckily outside the First Aid Hut.

The 400 set from 1979 contained the old faithful JPS Lotus Formula 1 car which had been produced for years, plus the six-wheel March which, unlike the six-wheel Tyrrell, had the two extra wheels at the back.

THE 1980s:
SENNA, MANSELL AND
MAGNATRACTION

THE BIRTH OF HORNBY HOBBIES

BY THE END of the 1970s Dunbee-Combex-Marx Ltd were struggling, just as Lines Bros had done a decade earlier, and in 1980 their assets too were sold off. This time, a management buyout saved the day and Hornby Hobbies Ltd was formed in 1980, taking over both Scalextric and Hornby model railways.

When Hornby Hobbies took over the brand, a lot of people wondered if they would carry on with the lack of adventure shown during the 1970s, or whether this might lead to a new 'golden age'. Thankfully it was to be the latter.

First of all, after a gap of nine years, some new Scalextric motorcycle combinations arrived. Gone were the spindly wheels and belt drives of the old Typhoon and Hurricane – the new designs had proper fat tyres and actually handled really well for their day, zooming up the straights and belting round the corners better than a lot of their four-wheeled counterparts.

STOCK CARS, BANGER RACERS AND TRUCKS

Some of the most popular cars like the TR7 went on and on into the 1980s both as part of the immensely popular 300 Set and also available on their own in various liveries. But there were also some new and innovative ideas coming along for the new decade, one of which was cars with bits that flew off on impact – otherwise known as 'stock cars' or 'Super Stox'.

The two Super Stox cars were called 'Stick Shifter' and 'Fender Bender'. They were designed so that when they hit each other, or anything else, parts such as the exhausts and bonnets fell off them. Having two cars that were meant to be crashed was great fun. Instead of having to get the glue out after a massive shunt had sent bits flying everywhere, all the pieces could simply be snapped back into place and the performance repeated all over again. The cars could also spin round and keep on driving, as could the Mini banger racers.

There must have been a lot of fun in the marketing office at that time while thinking up names for these new creations. The two Mini banger racers were called 'Mad Hatter' and 'Mini Ha-Ha'. These cars were great fun to drive.

Opposite:
The Brabham BT49 and the Saudia Leyland Williams attack the banking, although they didn't really need it: these cars were sensational in handling and looks.

The motorcycles and sidecars of 1980 in green and red. The can-type motors were mounted along the chassis and drove the back wheels through a crown gear and pinion.

Below:
'Stick Shifter' and 'Fender Bender', the two stock car racers which made their debut in 1981 in the Super Stox Set. Here they are, doing what they did best – crashing.

Below right:
Just one year later, banger racing was introduced, with two beaten-up Minis called 'Mad Hatter' and 'Mini Ha-Ha'.

Nothing actually fell off them when they crashed (at least, nothing was supposed to fall off), but they had pickups which could turn right round through 360 degrees and still function. This meant that you could launch your banger into a corner, do a 180-degree spin and carry on driving back the way you had come.

The guide had a blade at both front and rear and the braids that collect current from the track were fixed at both ends, so they could pick up electricity while running in either direction. The earliest braids used on the first plastic cars in the 1960s were mounted in the same way, although at that time they were not pivoted. The term 'loop-braids' is still used in discussions about the old Vanwalls, Astons, Jaguars and others of that period.

Truck racing arrived in 1982, with the worrying headline in Catalogue 23: 'A New Concept Demanding New Skills'. These were large trucks, with or without trailers, and really were too big to fit on the track, especially on

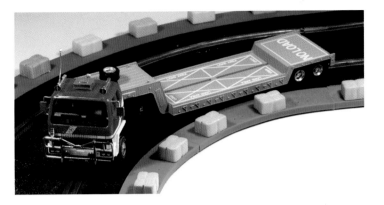

The Leyland low-loader complete with its shining chrome bull-bars, mirrors, air-horns and CB radio antenna. (The tailgate was often the first thing to go missing on these – and the example shown is no exception!)

tight bends. This was obviously where the new skills that had been forecast were needed – the description in the catalogue went on to say, 'Driving vehicles like these is not for the faint hearted'. Yes indeed! A year later a pair of tractor units called 'Racing Rigs' was announced. They looked completely ridiculous with V-shaped wings on the back.

FORMULA 1, RALLY AND SALOON CARS

In Formula 1, the Brabham and Williams teams were contesting most of the races (Ferrari were at the start of their lean period, which would not see them win a world title from 1979 with Scheckter to 2000 with Schumacher – a wait of twenty-one years). The Brabham team had been around since the 1960s and the great Jack Brabham was the first to win a race or a title in a car bearing his own name. Nelson Piquet won his first driver's title in 1981 in the BT49, then won again in 1983, thereby becoming the first ever driver to do so in a turbocharged car (the engine was a four-cylinder BMW which, incredibly, was based on a design from 1961). The Williams won the title with Alan Jones in 1980 and again in 1982 with Keke Rosberg. Both the Brabham and the Williams were produced by Scalextric for many years, and they handled superbly without the need for banking to keep them from flying off on the corners.

In 1981 Scalextric produced the first version of the Rover 3500 saloon car in its SD1 form (the first car produced by British Leyland's Specialist Division – hence SD1). Many different forms of this car with its striking shape were produced, including various police liveries, and a flamboyant black and yellow marshal's car with two chequered flags flying from the roof.

The red (1982) and white (1984) Capris are led gently into the bend by the Rover 3500 Marshal's car, which first appeared in 1984.

Audi Quattros were large cars – unlike the nimble Minis and Escorts of years gone by – but their four-wheel drive meant that they could take the corners at much higher speeds without even sliding.

Catalogue 23 had a whopping sixty-four pages – the most so far for any Scalextric catalogue. Catalogue 26 on the other hand had a mere eight pages. This was because (so the popular theory goes) the company had yet another financial crisis in 1984, which meant they put only the new releases into the 1985 catalogue. But among the re-liveried Porsches and Mini Metros in this curtailed brochure, one new release was worth waiting for – the amazing four-wheel-drive Audi Quattro, whose full-size contemporary was winning everything in the rally world. Of course, Scalextric wanted the model to be four-wheel-drive too, so they fitted pulleys to the front and rear axles and connected them up using rubber bands. As the front wheels were rarely in contact with the ground anyway, it didn't make any difference to the traction available – but when you spun the wheels up it looked great.

Unlike the Scalextric model which was owned by many boy-racers, the real-life Audi Quattro was out of the reach of 99 per cent of the population because of its cost. The Ford Escort XR3 – followed by the petrol injected XR3i – was just the opposite: here was a sporty Ford in the great tradition of RS2000s and Mexicos, and most people could afford one. The Scalextric XR3i came out in 1983, and from then on people could own both – one sitting on the road outside, the other flying down the straight, missing the corner and hitting the cat.

The Ford Escort XR3i, which was modelled by Scalextric in lots of different formats. The red one shown here is the earliest one, produced in 1983.

TURBOFLASH AND MAGNATRACTION

During the latter half of the 1980s, the Formula 1 scene was dominated by Prost, Piquet and Senna. However, because Scalextric is British and Nigel Mansell was always up with the leaders before crashing out, the new giant set of 1988 featured the best driver in the world at that time, Ayrton Senna, and the best British hope: the man with the funny moustache. It was also named after the circuit where the British Grand Prix was always held, Silverstone, and provided enough track to have a stab at building something which looked a bit like it.

But there was more. As if the sight of Mansell in his Williams Honda and Senna in his similarly-engined Lotus racing neck and neck was not enough to entice you to buy the Silverstone set, the cars had two new features, one of which made them handle better at higher speeds than any Scalextric car before. This was 'Magnatraction'. Mounted beneath each car was a small, light, permanent magnet that was positioned as close as possible to the conductor rails on the track, hovering just above but not touching them, and insulated by a thin plastic layer so that even if it did touch them, the electricity could not take a short circuit through the magnet. As with aerodynamic downforce on the real cars, the Scalextric cars now had downforce of their own provided by the magnet being attracted to the steel rails on the track. In practice this meant that it wasn't necessary to slow down so much for the corners, and the back end of the car did not slide out as with the old style of driving (although once it did slide out the magnet was removed from its proximity with the metal part of the track and the car lost half of its adhesion in an instant, causing a very high speed accident).

The other innovation on these cars was the result of a phenomenon that had been spotted by race watchers ever since Formula 1 cars had changed over to turbocharged engines. When the driver took his foot off the throttle coming into a bend the turbocharger, still spinning furiously, continued to pour petrol into the engine in large amounts which then collected in the exhaust. The red-hot manifold caused this fuel to catch fire and burn with a bright yellow flame streaking out of the rear of the car, accompanied by a cacophony of back-firing. The Scalextric version was called 'Turboflash'. It didn't reproduce the sounds of the spluttering engines, but what it did do was flicker a small amber LED on the back of the car when you took your finger off the hand controller at high speed. This was quite pretty if you drove with the curtains drawn and the lights out, but in daylight it was not that noticeable.

The Canon Williams Honda and the Camel Lotus Honda of 1988. Magnatraction made the cars stick to the circuit like glue. The later version of the pit has bright yellow tools.

THE 1990s AND BEYOND: STILL GOING STRONG

W E'VE ALREADY mentioned many developments of interest that occurred in the 1990s in the chapter on film and television – Batman, Mutant Hero Turtles, and so on. In 1991 there was also another attempt at Electric Horse Racing – this time a flat racing version – but this soon went the way of its steeple-chasing predecessor of 1970 even though it was 'endorsed by Willy Carson'.

Meanwhile, all the old favourites such as Mini Metros, Jaguar and Porsche Le Mans cars, Ford Sierra Cosworths, BMW M3s, Benetton, Tyrrell, Ferrari, Lotus, McLaren and Williams Formula 1 cars went on and on.

In 1991 the Easy Fit Guide Blade was launched, and soon all cars were equipped to take these devices. The idea was that instead of having the fiddly job of replacing the individual braids on the guide that was attached to the car, the whole assembly was detachable, held in place by two clips. To change the braids, you just pulled the worn one off, and pushed a new one on – it took just a few seconds and the cars were off and running again.

One of the new marques of Formula 1 car to come on strongly in the 1990s was the Benetton team. Reflecting the bright colours used by the team owners in their clothing products, the cars were very striking when they appeared in Scalextric form in 1990.

The 1994 Formula 1 season was a year of death and high drama on the circuits of the world, with Michael Schumacher in his number 5 Benetton Ford crashing into Damon Hill in the number 0 Rothmans Williams Renault at Adelaide in the final race of the series, thereby winning the title by one point. A Scalextric set was produced the following year containing both these cars, enabling racing enthusiasts around the world to re-live the moment. The most impressive rally cars of the time were the Subaru Imprezas, and these were turned into lovely models too.

A major upheaval in the 1990s was the transfer of all production to factories in China, as almost all consumer goods manufacturers were doing at that time. However, there was no noticeable change, except for the words on the floorpans of the cars themselves.

Opposite:
The Mighty Metros came along at the end of the 1980s and continued right through the 1990s. These were the most common cars for years, introducing many thousands of children to Scalextric, just as the old Formula Juniors had done in the 1960s.

Above:
Dapple grey horse 'Fairweather Lady' and sulky 'Julie's Choice' didn't inspire the crowds and were soon dropped.

Left:
A Scalextric re-creation of the infamous 'coming together' of Damon Hill in the number 0 Rothmans Williams Renault and Michael Schumacher in his number 5 Benetton Ford in the last race of the 1994 F1 season in Australia.

Two Subaru Imprezas – the great rally cars of the late '90s and early 2000s. The blue one is the standard Scalextric issue; the red one is a special limited edition for Gamleys.

If the 1990s were quiet in terms of development, the 2000s saw huge changes. The first of these was the track re-design and its launch in 2001. The new 'sport' track pushes together like the original rubber track of the 1950s, but when it is located it locks into place. The plastic 'classic' track first hit the shops in 1963 and therefore enjoyed an uninterrupted reign of thirty-eight years – it must have been quite a good design! The new track was certainly easier to take apart than the old, but it can be a struggle to line all four tabs up when pushing it together.

The Scalextric MotoGP bikes need a support each side to hold them up and look very silly while cornering as, not being able to lean, they wobble from side to side.

Within three years of the new track coming out, Scalextric Digital was released, whereby up to six cars can race independently on the same track, and they can change lanes using lane-changing tracks that operate like sets of points on a model railway. This system is compatible with the sport track, but needs a converter and obviously the extra track for lane-changing. The cars are fitted with an electronic decoder that listens out for the commands that apply to that particular car and then drive its motor accordingly, but they also work fine on normal track using the old analogue system.

The other change was to the layout of the drive-train of the cars. It seems almost incredible, but as with the new track reverting to the 1950s style of pushing together, so the motors were now mounted transversely at the back of the car, driving the rear wheels via plain gears with no crown wheel, just as did the original tinplate cars from almost fifty years before. The new motors were incredibly light, revving to 20, 25 or even 30 thousand rpm

— and yet they consumed far less electric current than the old RX motors of the 1960s — and a fraction of the massive two amps or so required by the old Race-tuned version.

In 2007, Scalextric celebrated its fiftieth birthday — there couldn't have been many people who remembered the unveiling at the Harrogate Toy Fair in 1957 half a century before. A commemorative badge was produced, and a book, and various special editions of cars and sets.

I hope you have enjoyed this trip through one of the highlights of our childhoods. We compiled our wish-lists, poring over the catalogue, ticking all the cars and bridges and buildings we desired. We then scoured the price list, totting up the total, and experienced the horrible realisation that it came to so much money that we would be lucky to be able to afford a tenth of it: another year of relentless saving loomed ahead. The pocket money would have to go straight into the Scalextric fund, no sweets and no treats while the piggy bank got heavier and heavier. The trip to the toy shop took a lifetime to arrive — but when it did, there was heaven. The money was strewn all over the counter and the shiny new car was safely popped into its carrier bag.

I also hope that we have presented a sufficiently large selection of cars for you to have owned a substantial number of them, and remember them with fondness. You will probably even recall which parts of them fell off, broke off, or otherwise; which colour schemes you painted them in; and the wheel-arches you cut away to fit wider tyres so they gripped better round the corners (that was always the theory — but did it really work?). Remember the braids wearing out and using the copper screen from TV aerial cable to make new ones at a fraction of the cost of the factory replacements? Those were the days. Here's to the next fifty years.

The Fiftieth Anniversary badge of 2007. Notice that the '50 years' is actually mounted onto a representation of a piece of track, complete with slots.

FURTHER READING

Chang, Dave. *The Slot Car Handbook*. The Crowood Press, 2007.

Gillham, Roger. *Scalextric: The Ultimate Guide*. J. H. Haynes & Co. Ltd, 2008.

Gillham, Roger. *Scalextric: A Race Through Time – The Official 50th Anniversary Book*. J. H. Haynes & Co. Ltd, 2007.

Green, Rob. *Scalextric: The Story of the World's Favourite Model Racing Cars*. Harper Collins Illustrated, 2001.

Van Den Abeele, Alain, and De Ville, Eric. *Scalextric History and Passion*. IHM Publishing, 1999.

For a comprehensive listing of all Scalextric cars consult
www.slotcarportal.com

To join a collectors' club visit the official Scalextric website at
www.scalextric.com or for slot-cars in general www.nscc.co.uk,
which has news and views and details of swapmeets where you can pick
up collectors' cars.

For the very latest news, tips and help on any make of slot-car visit the
forums on www.slotforum.com

INDEX

Page numbers in italics refer to illustrations and catalogue numbers for each model are shown in brackets